War ended in Europe on 7 May 1945. The Japanese went on fighting until August when America dropped two atom bombs on Japan ending WWII. The atom bombs were 2,000 times more powerful than the largest bomb dropped in the war.

dangers of a total war and you have shared no less in the triumph of the Allied Nations.

I know you will always feel proud to belong to a country which was capable of such supreme effort; proud, too, of parents and elder brothers and sisters who by their courage, endurance and enterprise brought victory. May these qualities be yours as you grow up and join in the common effort to establish among the nations of the world unity and peace.

George R.I.

When the war ended this message from King George VI was sent to all school children.

2

Protecting the seas

The Royal Navy fought at sea from warships and the Merchant Navy carried tools, oil and machines to and from Britain.

During the war, large numbers of merchant ships crossed the Atlantic Ocean carrying vital supplies to Britain from the USA. Hitler attacked them with U-boats (submarines) because he knew that without these supplies, Britain would not survive. Supply ships joined together to form 'convoys' protected by Royal Navy warships.

Vice-Admiral Ramsay had less than one week to plan 'Operation Dynamo' – the rescue of 300,000 troops trapped by the German army on the French coast.

HMS Belfast, a warship built in 1939.

The Royal Navy was involved in many battles with the German Navy. It used its own air force (the Fleet Air Arm) to attack the enemy from the air. Aircraft took off and landed back on aircraft carriers and from shore naval airbases.

Lookout!

Look out for HMS Belfast on the River Thames in London and HMS Cavalier at Chatham Historic Dockyard, Kent. Find out what you score on page 14.

4

Defending the land

Soldiers fighting for Britain fought in Europe, in the deserts of North Africa and in the jungles of Burma and Malaya.

Shorts or ski wear this time?

Soldiers fought with guns, grenades, landmines and tanks but there was very little hand-to-hand fighting. When soldiers were not fighting, they helped to put out fires, defuse bombs and clear up bomb damage.

Lookout!

Look out for a tank in an army museum. Find out what you score on page 14.

5

Field Marshal Montgomery (Monty) commanded the British Army in the deserts of North Africa. After two years of fierce fighting, his army defeated the enemy at El Alamein in Egypt. It was the first great victory on land for the Allies (countries fighting on the same side as Britain).

The lads from our street

Pictures like this appeared in newspapers to keep everyone's spirits up.

Highly trained Royal Marines fought on land, at sea or in the sky. They manned landing craft, drove tanks and flew with the Fleet Air Arm.

COMMANDO

Q: What do you call a sheep with a machine gun?

A: Lambo!

6

Attacking from the air

The Royal Air Force (RAF) used aircraft to drop bombs, to shoot down German aircraft and to photograph the positions, activities and buildings of the enemy.

WILLS'S CIGARETTES

GLOUCESTER GAUNTLET
INTERCEPTOR FIGHTERS

A cigarette card showing fighter planes.

Lookout!

Look out for WWII aircraft in museums about the air force. Find out what you score on page 14.

Douglas Bader was a WWII hero. He had lost both legs in a flying accident before the war but still became a fighter pilot with the RAF. He brought down lots of enemy aircraft – and without legs!

Bomber planes carried a team of about six airmen. A pilot flew the plane while a navigator followed the route and operated the radio. Others dropped the bombs and fired machine guns at enemy aircraft.

Q: What do you get if you jump out of a plane without a parachute?

A: Shorter!

Aircraft were also used to give cover to troops on the ground, to parachute spies into enemy country and to drop supplies in places under attack.

8

Secrets and spies

During the war both sides employed spies to find out what the enemy was planning. If spies were captured they were usually tortured or shot.

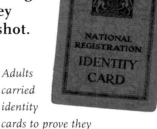

In Britain, many spies worked for the Special Operations Executive (SOE). They operated in enemy territory carrying simple equipment for spying, armed only with a revolver and a knife.

Adults carried identity cards to prove they weren't German spies!

Q: What do you call a spy when he goes to bed?

A: An undercover agent!

Both sides in the war used codes to send secret messages. At Bletchley Park, near Milton Keynes, mathematicians developed an early type of computer to decipher German codes. Valuable information then fell into Britain's hands.

Lookout!

Look out for code-breaking machines at Bletchley Park. Find out what you score on page 14.

When you get home …

… decipher this code! Unjumble the words to find out the name of the famous code machine used by Germans to send messages. The code was deciphered at Bletchley Park. It was an exceptionally difficult task because the codes changed every day!

TEH _ ~ _ ~

GNIAEM ~ _ ~ ~ | ~

CEDO _ ~ ~ ~

MAIHNCE _ ~ _ ~ ~ ~

Answer: The Enigma Code Machine

10

Women in uniform

Women could choose to join the armed forces such as the Women's Auxiliary Air Force (WAAF), the Women's Royal Naval Service (WRNS) and the Auxiliary Territorial Service (ATS). But they were not allowed to fight.

Women in the ATS became army nurses, drove trucks and kept watch for enemy attacks.

These women belonged to the ATS.